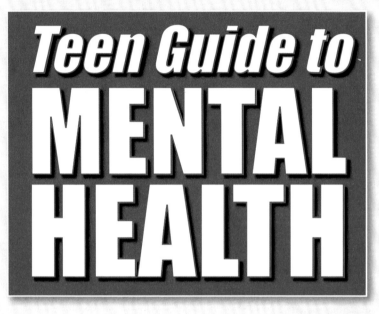

Teen Guide to MENTAL HEALTH

Don Nardo

ReferencePoint
Press®

San Diego, CA

For more information, contact:
ReferencePoint Press, Inc.
PO Box 27779
San Diego, CA 92198
www.ReferencePointPress.com

LIBRARY OF CONGRESS CATALOGING-IN-PUBLICATION DATA

Names: Nardo, Don, 1947– author.
Title: Teen Guide to Mental Health/by Don Nardo.
Description: San Diego, CA: ReferencePoint Press, Inc., 2020. | Audience:
  Grade 9 to 12. | Includes bibliographical references and index.
Identifiers: LCCN 2019018536 (print) | LCCN 2019018780 (ebook) | ISBN
  9781682827543 (eBook) | ISBN 9781682827536 (hardback)
Subjects: LCSH: Teenagers—Mental health—Juvenile literature. |
  Teenagers—Social conditions—Juvenile literature. | Body image—Juvenile
  literature.
Classification: LCC RJ503 (ebook) | LCC RJ503 .N357 2020 (print) | DDC
  618.92/89—dc23
LC record available at https://lccn.loc.gov/2019018536

CONTENTS

Stress Among Teens Is on the Rise

"I'm kinda hard on myself," says a teenager named Rachel. "Like I feel really bad if I don't have a 4.0 grade average." Another teen, named Tim, is not worried about grades. Rather, he says he worries about "making new friends without ex-friends spreading rumors." Relationships also concern fourteen-year-old Lolo, who complains, "My best friend left last year, and I'm worried about who I'll hang out with." Amina, who is in the same grade as Lolo, says, "There are these really jealous girls and they are always stressing me out."[1]

Other teens have problems with parents or siblings, while still others are anxious because they are gay and find it hard to fit into a social scene in which certain stigmas against gay people are common. Other groups of young people are repeatedly bullied, suffer from depression or an eating disorder, or have become addicted to drugs. In fact, experts on mental health point out that a majority of today's teens feel some level of stress, anxiety, or upset over one or more aspects of their lives. According to a 2018 study of US teens ages thirteen to seventeen, conducted by the widely respected Pew Research Center,

> Anxiety and depression are on the rise among America's youth and, whether they personally suffer from these conditions or not, seven-in-ten teens today see them as major problems among their peers. Concern about mental health cuts across gender, racial and socio-economic lines, with roughly equal shares of teens across demographic groups saying it is a significant issue in their community.[2]

Sources of Teenage Worries

The worries at the top of the list for teens relate to school and friends. According to the Pew study, of the numerous possible sources of stress or anxiety for teens, the single most prevalent one consists of worries surrounding grades. About 61 percent of those surveyed said they felt a lot of pressure—from parents, teachers, and/or themselves—to do as well as possible in academic pursuits. Meanwhile, about three in ten teens said they felt a certain amount of pressure to look good and fit in socially, both at school and within their peer groups.

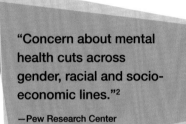

"Concern about mental health cuts across gender, racial and socio-economic lines."[2]

—Pew Research Center

Many other concerns also trouble teens. Fully half of the teens surveyed pointed out that overconsumption of alcohol and drug addiction are serious problems among the teens in their communities; in addition, 6 percent said they felt undue pressure to drink alcohol even when they did not want to, and 4 percent said they had been pressured by friends to take illegal drugs. At the same time, 23 percent of the respondents said they worried daily about whether their parents would be able to make enough money to keep paying all the bills. Another 7 percent said that, regardless of their financial situations at home, most of their stress came from them frequently being in trouble with law enforcement.

Other similar sources of teenage worries and stress were revealed by data collected in 2018 by the American Psychological Association (APA). This survey also singled out the various ways that teens tend to react to and deal with their worries and stress. A surprisingly high proportion—35 percent—of the several thousand teens questioned reported lying awake at night, overeating, or eating unhealthy foods in reaction to the stresses they felt in their lives. Fully 40 percent said they felt angry fairly often. Another 36 percent described feeling nervous or uneasy on a regular basis, and the same proportion—36 percent—said they felt overly

US Teens Worry About Anxiety and Depression

A majority of US teens considers anxiety and depression to be a major problem for their age group, according to a 2019 Pew Research Center survey of youth aged thirteen to seventeen. Seven in ten teens say these conditions represent a serious concern, even if they themselves do not experience anxiety or depression. Depression and anxiety rank higher even than bullying and drug addiction among teen concerns.

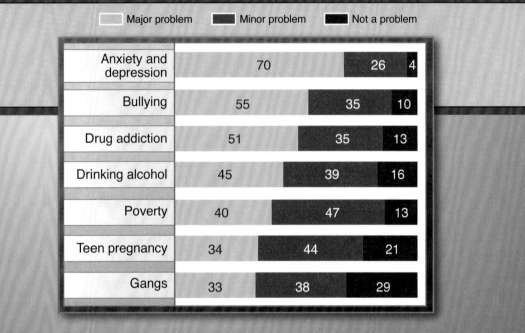

Anxiety and Depression Top List of Problems Teens See Among Their Peers

Percentage of teens saying each of the following is a _____ among people their age in the community where they live

	Major problem	Minor problem	Not a problem
Anxiety and depression	70	26	4
Bullying	55	35	10
Drug addiction	51	35	13
Drinking alcohol	45	39	16
Poverty	40	47	13
Teen pregnancy	34	44	21
Gangs	33	38	29

Note: Share of respondents who did not offer an answer is not shown.

Source: Pew Research Center, Juliana M. Menasce Horowitz and Nikki Graf, "Most U.S. Teens See Anxiety and Depression as a Major Problem Among Their Peers," February 20, 2019. www.pewsocialtrends.org.

tired one or more times per week. Particularly revealing was the finding that half of the teens in the study said that at least once a month someone tells them they appear to be stressed out.

Considering these and other facts, the mental health therapist who reported the APA study's findings online, Kathleen Smith, remarks that many teens "struggle with significant stress levels

that interfere with learning, relationships, and other areas of functioning."
She adds, "stress can manifest in different ways, and some symptoms of
stress mimic normal teen behavior. To
that end, stress can sneak up on teens.
It's important to know what to look for when it comes to teen
stress."[3] Stress can manifest itself in a number of ways, Smith
writes, including emotional changes, such as frequent displays
of anxiety and depression. There can also be physical changes,
which can include frequent headaches or stomachaches; behavioral changes, including poor eating or sleeping habits; and
cognitive changes, such as diminished ability to concentrate or
remember simple things.

Just Part of Growing Up?

Today's teens are not the first generation of young people to feel
various forms of stress. Moreover, experiencing a certain amount
of stress is actually a normal part of growing up. Indeed, says
family psychotherapist Katie Hurley, "all kids encounter stress of
varying degrees as they grow." She adds, "Despite their best ef-
forts, parents can't protect kids from obstacles. Kids get sick,
move to new neighborhoods, encounter bullies, take tests, cope
with grief, lose friends, and deal with divorce, to name a few."[4]

Still, as Hurley and other experts point out, studies indicate
clearly that modern teens are experiencing higher levels of stress
than earlier generations did. Furthermore, as the Pew Research
Center states, "anxiety and depression are on the rise among
America's youth."[5] For these reasons, taking a closer look at selected aspects of teenagers' lives that can and do sometimes
affect their mental health is warranted.

CHAPTER ONE

Balancing Home and School

The two principal settings that modern teenagers inhabit are their homes, where they live with parents and siblings or other family members, and school, the central focus of their education and social life. Traditionally, those two spheres are intertwined in a number of ways. Moreover, the average teen hopes to be productive and achieve stability and happiness in both home life and school life. That goal is not always easy to achieve, because in fulfilling their responsibilities in both spheres, teens inevitably encounter various pressures and sources of stress. In the words of Nancy Brown of California's Palo Alto Medical Foundation, "Although most teens may not be holding down full-time jobs, they are still under a lot of pressure from their daily responsibilities, and can benefit from finding a healthy balance. School, extracurricular activities, sports, part-time jobs, and responsibilities at home can cause a teen's life to feel like a juggling act."[6]

Family Discord and Pressures

Experts on teenagers' mental health point out that each young person is unique, as are his or her life experiences, personal goals, and levels of productivity and success in navigating home life and school life. Similarly, the sources of stress on some teens can be quite different from those that affect other teens. Nevertheless, studies, including the previously mentioned study conducted in 2018 by the APA, reveal that there are some fairly common sources of pressure and stress within the teen population.

The APA study and other compara-ble surveys looked first at teens' home lives, including relationships with par-ents and siblings. Not surprisingly, the findings indicated that family discord is a primary source of stress of one kind or another for many teens. Kathleen Smith,

"Stress trickles down, and anything that impacts the family can affect the teen."[7]

—Mental health therapist Kathleen Smith

who reported the results of the APA study, explains that "stress trickles down, and anything that impacts the family can affect the teen. Unrealistic expectations, marital problems, strained sibling relationships, illness in the family, and financial stress on the family can all trigger a spike in teen stress."[7]

One of the most common forms of family-generated stress on teens consists of parents exerting undue pressure on their chil-dren to achieve and succeed in both school and life in general. "Parents are the worst about all of this," Illinois high school stu-dent Colin told researchers who were looking into how stress af-fects teens. "All I hear is, 'Work harder, you're a smart kid, I know you have it in you, and if you want to go to college you need to work harder.' It's a pain."[8]

In that same study a young woman named Elizabeth, who was attending high school in Texas, had a different type of pa-rental complaint. "My mom recently got a new job," she said. "So one big thing that's stressing me out is how I have to do even more chores at home now. I like to help my parents [but] some-times there aren't enough hours in the day to wash dishes, do laundry, help my little brother with homework, do my own home-work, and study."[9]

Abuse in the Home

It turns out that both Colin and Elizabeth were fortunate in one way. Although they felt a certain amount of stress because their parents were strict or demanding, they suffered no physical or emotional abuse. The exact percentage of teens who suffer such

Teens experience a lot of different pressures. Schoolwork, planning for college, making friends, worries about family finances, and even extra household chores can all build up and lead to added stress.

abuses in the home each year is unknown. But in 2018 the American Academy of Pediatrics estimated that roughly 5.5 million young people, many of them teenagers, are abused by parents and/or siblings each year.

Such abuse clearly generates a lot of stress among the teens involved. Moreover, evidence from a 2016 study reported in the *International Journal of Pediatrics and Adolescent Medicine* suggests that this sort of mistreatment actually subtly damages the victims' brains. Also, even when the abuse is only verbal, the young person on the receiving end feels its negative effects in other areas of life, including school and relationships with other teens. Indeed, according to science writer Peg Streep, "Verbal abuse and aggression doesn't take place in a vacuum—it poisons the family well and the springs that feed it."[10]

Academic and Other School-Related Stresses

Among those teens whose home lives are *not* major sources of stress, a great many make up for it at school. In fact, in its broad-based 2018 study of teen stress, the Pew Research Center found that more than 60 percent of American teens feel some sort of academic-related stress on a regular basis. Such stress has different causes, including the expectations of teachers and parents, pressure to get good grades, nervousness about taking important exams, and/or feeling overtaxed by too much homework.

California teen Sargunjot often feels overwhelmed by these kinds of burdens. "It's like a pressure cooker in here!" she says about her high school environment, adding, "No doubt, school is tough. For some, it's the worry of being able to get enough credits to graduate high school, while for others it's being able to get a 4.0 GPA [grade point average] and get into Stanford. No matter what our goals are, we all struggle with a tremendous amount of stress and pressure."[11]

A sixteen-year-old Seattle teen, Bretta, says she also feels school-related stress. "Academic stress has been a part of my life ever since I can remember," she states. "This year I spend about 12 hours a day on schoolwork. I'm home right now because I was feeling so sick from stress I couldn't be at school. So as you can tell, it's a big part of my life!"[12] Schoolwork is frequently only one aspect of school-related pressures on teens. Some young people go out for sports teams. Others get involved in different extracurricular activities, among them clubs, the school newspaper, and student plays and talent shows.

In terms of the numbers of young people involved, sports is the single biggest school-sponsored extracurricular activity that teens pursue. Just as the strong urge to do well in one's academic subjects can cause feelings of stress in a teenager, so too can the desire to perform well in one's chosen sport. Interestingly, only a minority of teens who join sports teams allow those pursuits to get in the way of their academic work. According to sociologist Jay J. Coakley, "Studies have shown consistently that when compared with students who do not play varsity sports, high school athletes, as a group, generally have better grade point averages, more positive attitudes towards school, more interest in continuing their education after graduation, and a slightly better educational achievement rate."[13]

"High school athletes, as a group, generally have better grade point averages, [and] more positive attitudes towards school."[13]

—Sociologist Jay J. Coakley

Balancing Academics and Sports

The natural question is how so many high school athletes are able to achieve an effective balance between their sports activities and academic work. The answer, experts on teen mental health point out, is that they learn to be as organized as possible. One method these experts recommend is to buy a large desk calendar devoted just to schoolwork and one's chosen sport. The student writes down all known due dates for school-related exams, papers, and special projects. She or he also records all sports practice sessions and games.

The person then makes sure to check the calendar every day, as well as look at dates for each upcoming week in advance. Knowing, for example, that a big game and an important history paper are both due in six days, the person can effectively budget his or her time during those days and make sure to be fully prepared for both deadlines. "Look at your calendar and note when you have projects due, tests scheduled, and practices and games scheduled," advises Jeanne Goodes, who coaches teen baseball teams in Lake Zurich, Illinois. "Plan *how* you will study and *when* you will study. Use your weekends wisely. Use your weekend as preparation time for the week ahead. Start homework for the up-coming week. Read chapters and take notes ahead of time."[14] Goodes also advises devoting part of each weekend to doing some schoolwork ahead of schedule and using all free periods and study halls in one's school week to catch up on any homework or school papers one is behind on.

High school runners vie for the prize in a 3000-meter race. Although balancing academics and sports can be difficult at times, many teen athletes demonstrate strong academic achievement.

A Scary Wake-Up Call

Stress over supposedly normal things like managing home life and school can sometimes build up and affect young people in ways they neither expect nor understand. That stress can manifest itself not only in emotional ways but also in physical ways. For instance, an eighteen-year-old Illinois high school student named Hannah recalls a scary incident during her senior year:

> I had a really difficult time with stress last year. I was in the middle of switching friend groups and college applications were just around the corner. During my first round of finals, I noticed my right wrist going numb, but I didn't think much of it. Within a couple of months, it was numb practically all the time; on two occasions, I couldn't feel my entire left arm or part of my face. I didn't even have enough control over my hand to text my dad that this was happening! I went to my doctor who explained that I was carrying my stress in my shoulders. They had become so tight that my vertebrae were pushed forward, cutting off the nerve endings and causing me to lose feeling. That was a wakeup call—I couldn't keep doing this to myself.

Quoted in Alexandra Thurmond, "Under Pressure: Teens Speak Out About Stress," *Teen Vogue*, March 17, 2014. www.teenvogue.com.

The Cyberspace Factor

Budgeting one's time efficiently does more than help balance a person's schoolwork and extracurricular activities. Becoming better organized overall also helps balance school life with home life. This is because most of the time that a teenager spends outside of school is spent at home. So getting on an efficient schedule of doing homework automatically coordinates some school hours with home hours.

In addition, another potent factor now connects teenagers' supposedly private home lives to school and other sectors of the outside world, in the process making their private lives far less private. That factor is cyberspace, particularly in the form of social media. Before the advent of cell phones and the Internet, a teen's home life was distinctly separate from the hours she or he spent at school, at a job, or going out with friends. Today, in contrast, most teens use their cell phones to bring the outside world into their private spaces. "Back in the day," remarks Los Angeles clinical social worker Linda Esposito, "we got a break from our peers after school and on the weekends. But now kids are on social media all day long."[15]

Moreover, that breach of privacy that is by default part of modern social media has created still another source of stress for teens. Many of them regularly find themselves worrying about the image they project through their cell phones. A 2016–2018 survey conducted by Britain's Royal Society for Public Health asked thousands of young people how social media platforms impacted their health and well-being. A majority of the teens responded that using Facebook, Twitter, and other social media increased their existing feelings of anxiety. Furthermore, many of the respondents said that connecting to people through those media increased rather than decreased feelings of depression and loneliness. As CNN correspondent Kelly Wallace puts it:

> "[Using a lot of] social media and advanced technology mean more distractions for kids and less time to truly unplug."[16]
>
> —CNN correspondent Kelly Wallace

Today's teens, unlike when I was growing up, can now compare their academic performance and everything else about their existence to other teens 24 hours a day through updates on Facebook, Twitter, Snapchat, you name the social network, and that only increases the stress. [All that] social media and advanced technology mean more distractions for kids and less time to truly unplug.[16]

Trying to Reduce Stress

The added pressures of social media at least partly explain why modern teens are overall more stressed-out than teens were in prior generations. Indeed, Kathleen Smith writes, the average teen experiences a combination of pressures from family and home life, school obligations, and the social media that often connect those two spheres. It is no wonder, she says, that "teen stress rivals that of adults."[17] This reality requires teens to learn strategies for reducing the impact of stress.

One of those strategies, says the Palo Alto Medical Foundation's Nancy Brown, is to begin setting priorities. That is, to help reduce stress, a teenager should sit down and try to determine the activities and goals that are most important in his or her life at that point in time. Enjoying stability on the home front and getting

Social media has a strong presence in the lives of most teens. It enhances connections between people but also makes it nearly impossible to maintain any separation between home life, school, and social life.

Social Media and Sleep Loss in Teens

A 2016–2018 study by Britain's Royal Society for Public Health found a strong link between teens' use of social media, especially in the home at bedtime, and an unhealthy lack of sleep. "Sleep is particularly important for teens and young adults," the study's final report concludes, because "the brain is not fully developed until a person is well into their twenties." Also, poor sleep is linked to several physical and mental health problems, including high blood pressure, obesity, and depression. The report continues:

> Increased social media use has a significant association with poor sleep quality in young people. Using social media on phones, laptops, and tablets at night before bed is also linked with poor quality sleep. . . . The use of LED lights before sleep can interfere with and block natural processes in the brain that trigger feelings of sleepiness, . . . [so] individuals end up getting fewer hours of sleep every night. One in five young people say they wake up during the night to check messages on social media, leading them to be three times more likely to feel constantly tired at school than their classmates who don't use social media during the night.

Royal Society for Public Health, *Status of Mind: Social Media and Young People's Mental Health and Wellbeing.* www.rsph.org.uk.

decent grades in school will almost certainly be high on the list. Playing a sport, acting in a school play, or spending more time with a girlfriend or boyfriend might also be in the mix. The list of priorities will, of course, differ from person to person.

The next step, Brown says, is to decide which of the listed activities can be realistically accomplished on a regular basis without the teen in question becoming too tired and overly stressed. "Do not be an over-achiever," she advises. "Being well-rounded is important. However, you do not need to be the captain of the football team, the lead in the school play, and employee of the month. Choose one or two activities that you can enjoy while also getting your school work done and having time to relax or visit with friends."[18]

Having decided how big a workload to take on, the teen can set some goals for the following two weeks or maybe the following month. The trick, Brown says, is to learn to set goals that can be achieved with a minimum amount of pressure and stress. Indeed, one of the biggest causes of stress for teens, Brown points out, is too much multitasking, or trying to do too many things at once. Another expert, former University of California professor Toni Bernhard, agrees. She remembers being a major overachiever and multitasker as a teen and young adult. "Call me a recovering multitasker," she jokes. "I've discovered that it takes a lot of discipline to break the habit, so much in fact, that sometimes I have to be content with 'less multitasking.' But it's a start."[19]

CHAPTER TWO

Friendship and Dating

Among the more common life experiences of the teenage years are those involving friendships and dating and the quite normal emotions and stresses associated with them. "The teenage years are a time of physical, emotional, and social growth and change," one expert points out. Also, "these changes don't happen at the same time, or at the same speed, from one person to the next." This is because "some people are naturally outgoing and have no trouble making friends. Others are more shy and find it harder to get to know people."[20]

Regardless of what age a teen may be when she or he starts forming close relationships with peers, however, all teens sooner or later form such attachments. Many of these ties never end up developing past the "just friends" stage. But some relationships do result in dating. Of the teens who do date, some will fall in love, or at least be convinced that has happened. In fact, says a spokesperson for the American Academy of Pediatrics, "love is a subject of unending fascination for adolescents. Topping their list of questions is, 'How do you know when you're in love with somebody?'"[21]

> "Love is a subject of unending fascination for adolescents."[21]
>
> —A spokesperson for the American Academy of Pediatrics

Whether teen friendships remain casual or end up involving love, those relationships are key to young people's development of normal, positive mental health and happiness. "Teen friendships help young people feel a sense of acceptance and belonging," according to Newport Academy, a treatment center for teens with depression, anxiety, and other mental health issues. "Moreover, teenage relationships with peers support the development of compassion, caring, and empathy. Furthermore, adolescent friendships are a big part of forming a sense of identity outside the family."[22] No less important is the fact that teens who have close friendships are overall happier. A 2017 University of Virginia study found that teenagers with at least a few trusted friends enjoy better mental health and are far less likely to suffer from depression or anxiety than teens who do not form these friendships.

The Value of Friendship

The same study looked at the reasons why having a close friendship can make a teen feel more stable and happy. First and foremost, as might be expected, this happens because a person tends to build strong feelings of trust with a good friend. One can share important experiences and personal secrets with him or her, which provides both parties with a sense of belonging and self-worth.

The value of friendship also stems from the fact that both parties invest a good deal of time and effort in forming the friendship, says Jeffrey Hall, a professor at the University of Kansas. A 2018 study he conducted on how long it takes young people to form close bonds of friendship revealed that on average, two young people require about fifty hours of time together before considering themselves to be casual friends.

Some casual friendships remain just that, Hall found, mainly because one or both parties fail to devote the considerable amount of time to reach the next level. Indeed, it takes an average of another 290 hours, spread over the course of months, Hall discovered, for the two people to move from casual friends to close friends. A teenager or other young person absolutely must "put that time in," he states. "You can't snap your fingers and make a friend. Maintaining close relationships is the most important work we do in our lives."[23]

> "Maintaining close relationships is the most important work we do in our lives."[23]
>
> —University of Kansas professor Jeffrey Hall

The process of forming friendships contributes to the development of empathy and identity. Additionally, teens who have close friendships are overall happier than teens who do not.

Early Dating in Groups

Hall and other modern researchers surmise that when the parents of today's teens were teenagers themselves, developing close friendships took no less time and effort. Moreover, enjoying such close relationships with one or more peers was just as crucial to a teen's stability and happiness. What is very different today, studies show, is the manner in which modern teens differentiate between someone who is a "nondating" friend and a full-fledged boyfriend or girlfriend.

First, as Colorado pediatrician Ron Eagar points out, many teens today claim to be dating at ages far younger than in prior generations. In those days, he explains, adolescents more often than not waited till age fifteen, sixteen, or even seventeen to start getting "serious" with someone. In comparison, Eagar says, it is not unusual for modern teens to begin dating, on average, at ages twelve and a half for girls and thirteen and a half for boys.

However, Eagar and other experts caution, this claim to be dating by individuals just entering their teens can be deceiving.

Why Do Teens Use Social Media So Much?

One of the main reasons that modern teens use social media so regularly is that they feel this use benefits them in various ways. This was a key finding in a 2018 survey of almost one thousand American teenagers conducted by the Pew Research Center. According to Pew researchers Monica Anderson and Jingjing Jiang:

> Roughly eight-in-ten teens ages 13 to 17 (81%) say social media makes them feel more connected to what's going on in their friends' lives, while around two-thirds say these platforms make them feel as if they have people who will support them through tough times. And by relatively substantial margins, teens tend to associate their social media use with positive rather than negative emotions, such as feeling included rather than excluded (71% vs. 25%) or feeling confident rather than insecure (69% vs. 26%).

> Young people also believe social media helps teens become more civic minded and exposes them to greater diversity, either through the people they interact with or the viewpoints they come across. Roughly two-thirds of teens say these sites help people their age interact with individuals from diverse backgrounds, find different points of view, or show their support for causes or issues.

Monica Anderson and Jingjing Jiang, "Teens' Social Media Habits and Experiences," Pew Research Center, November 28, 2018. www.pewinternet.org.

Younger teens today often use the term *dating* to describe what adolescents in the past called "hanging out with my friends." The widespread custom is now for younger teens of both genders to socialize and date as part of a group. For example, four, five, six, or more teens will go to the mall or the movies together. Some may pair off for a while during the outing, but in a sense the others act as chaperones. "The number-one benefit is safety,"[24] Eagar says—not only physical safety but also emotional safety. This sort of "group dating" allows very young girls and boys to enjoy one another's company without the clumsiness and sexual tension that would exist if two teens that age went on a more traditional date.

Teen Romances and Breakups

Eventually, some teens do progress to that more traditional one-on-one style of dating, in which the two parties feel varying levels of affection for and/or commitment to each other. Mental health experts warn parents, teachers, and other adults in the lives of such committed teens not to casually dismiss the love the teens profess as "puppy love," "just a crush," or "not real love." The feelings those teens experience are genuine. "Even 14- and 15-year-olds can fall in love," asserts Crystal Reardon, director of counseling for North Carolina's Wake County Public School System. "To a child or teenager who is experiencing this, it is very real and very important,"[25] she says. Arizona pediatrician George Comerci agrees. "Parents should never minimize or ridicule a first love," he writes. "It is a very important relationship to teenagers, and it's important for another reason, in that it is their first intimate relationship with someone outside their family."[26]

A common by-product of teen romances in which the two people express their love for each other is a so-called broken heart, if and when the relationship ends. "Just as with adults, there's no timetable for recovery,"[27] says *Carolina Parent* magazine's Suzanne M. Wood. Following a breakup with a boyfriend or girlfriend, she explains, one or both parties may display signs of sadness, sleep deprivation, or depression for weeks or even months. In extreme cases, their grades may slip or they may quit a sport or other extracurricular activity.

Some idea of the depth of negative feelings that the breakup of a teen romance can generate comes from a fifteen-year-old New Mexico high school student named Poiema. She recalls:

> I invested so much of my time, my energy, and myself into something I thought was going to work, but then my boyfriend broke up with me. Heartbreak is literally the worst feeling in the world, and it's turned my entire existence upside down. Right after it happened, I had no idea who I was or what made me happy anymore. As I was losing myself in all these emotions, it was easy for me to get stressed out by school and other things in my life."[28]

Group outings are a popular way to have fun, but some teens eventually begin dating as couples. Relationships between couples can be uplifting but also heartbreaking if and when they end.

Teens Having Sex

Another fairly common by-product of high school romances consists of sexual activities. Sex among young people has long been a concern of parents, school authorities, and teens themselves because it can lead to unwanted consequences. Among them are accidental pregnancies, teens dropping out of school to care for unplanned children, and contracting sexually transmitted diseases (STDs).

The good news for all involved is that these negative outcomes are all on the decline in the United States because fewer of today's teens are having sex than teens in prior generations did. The results of a major national survey on teenage sex conducted by the Centers for Disease Control and Prevention (CDC) were released in 2017. The study showed that about 40 percent of boys and girls have sexual intercourse by age eighteen. That is an enormous decline from the peak in teen sexual activity in 1988, when 57 percent of teens aged fifteen to nineteen had engaged in sexual intercourse at least once.

Moreover, the CDC study indicated that the steepest declines in teen sex occurred from 2013 to 2015. The researchers who ran the survey reported that several different factors appear to have brought about this trend. The biggest single one, they said, was an Obama administration directive to give teens access to new sex-related curriculum in high schools and online. It consisted of honest, factual information about sexual relations, the negative consequences of teens having those relations, and the various methods of contraception. (The curriculum, which is still in place, strongly urges teens to refrain from having sex, but it also stresses the importance of using contraception if they do decide to engage in sexual intercourse, in order to avoid pregnancy and STDs.)

LGBT Teen Relationships

The 2017 CDC study included information mainly about sexual trends among heterosexual, or straight, teens. LGBT teens were unrepresented, in part because an unknown number of them are still not open about their orientation, a situation routinely called being "in the closet." As for how many teens are LGBT, no one knows for sure. Scientific estimates range from as low as 4 or 5 percent to more than 10 percent of the teen population. The most widely accepted figure in 2019 was that of noted demographer Gary J. Gates—about 7 percent, or about 3 million of the country's roughly 43 million teens.

These teens may experience different patterns of friendship and dating than straight teens, partly because it is harder for them to connect with each other. Although the stigma associated with being LGBT is not as strong as it once was and young people are coming out at earlier ages than ever before, forming relationships can be difficult for LGBT teens. "One of the areas where LGBT teens can get especially short-changed is in the dating department," says noted gay activist and writer Tony Bravo. He adds that "it can still be harder for LGBT youth to find one another and connect, and they can miss the formative teen romance rites of passage."[29]

Moreover, LGBT teens face various pressures that can make it difficult for them to form friendships at school. A 2018 nationwide study of about twelve thousand LGBT youth aged thirteen to seventeen found that only 26 percent feel safe at school. According to the 2018 Youth Report conducted by the Human Rights Campaign Foundation and researchers at the University of Connecticut, these young people experience harassment, rejection, bullying, and isolation—all of which affect their well-being and ability to develop close ties to peers.

Despite the challenges, many LGBT teens are able to make friends and be comfortable in their own skin. Aiding them are a growing number of LGBT-friendly clubs, both inside and outside high schools across the country. These groups give members a chance to socialize with other LGBT teens. In addition, a number

Friendships and romance can pose difficulties for LGBT youth. Despite the challenges, many LGBT teens are able to make friends and be comfortable in their own skin.

How Sexting Destroyed a Person's Life

In October 2012 a fifteen-year-old teen from British Columbia, Canada—Amanda Michelle Todd—took her own life due to extreme shame and stress caused by a series of sexting incidents. Her sad story, which shows one of the potential dangers of sexting, is summarized here by her mother, Carol Todd.

It all started with a topless photo. She didn't know the person at the other end of her computer was taking a picture. She didn't know that he was showing it to other men. Then she started to get blackmailed into showing more of herself via her webcam. And if she didn't, then her image would be sent throughout the Internet. What Amanda didn't do was tell an adult that this was happening to her. She kept it to herself. This image and what happened thereafter was the start to the emotional breakdown of Amanda. The loss of her confidence, her spirit and her friends. The embarrassment that followed was unbearable as was the name-calling, the slut-shaming and the bullying online and offline that occurred. Eventually Amanda retreated into a shell, not being able to re-emerge as the girl she once was. As a parent and Amanda's mother, it is important to me that young people understand what can happen online and also how to protect themselves online.

Quoted in Common Sense Education, "Send Me a Nudie?. . . Promise Not to Share?," 2015. www.commonsense media.org.

of websites now specialize in helping LGBT teens meet and/or date young people from their peer group.

Connecting Through Social Media

Whether a teen is straight, gay, bisexual, or transgender, he or she will likely employ most of the same friendship and dating customs, including meeting during or after school, going to school dances, and so forth. Another of those customs is the use of social media, including platforms like Instagram and Facebook. In 2018 the research organization Common Sense Media published a study of teen use of social media and found that the three most popular social media platforms they use are Snapchat, Instagram, and Facebook, in that order.

Furthermore, some of what teens call dating takes place online. Statista, a company that collects the results of recent social surveys and studies, reported in 2019 that 20 percent of teens have found at least one dating partner using social media. Other surveys show that almost half of those teens have told someone online that they liked or loved them. Also, about a third said they sometimes flirt with someone through social media.

Social media interactions often end up being just one aspect of healthy budding relationships, but these interactions can also go awry. Teen sexting, which involves sending someone a nude or partially nude photo of oneself via the Internet, might sound like fun, but it can have dire effects. Experts warn that even when the receiver assures the sender that the pictures will remain private, they rarely do. A majority of receivers—girls and boys alike—end up sharing them with other teens, and some of the photos end up on national dating or porn sites. Despite warnings by public health experts and others, teen sexting has become widespread. "Sexting is an increasingly common practice, with the prevalence increasing each year until youth reach the age of 18 years,"[30] say the authors of a 2018 study conducted by the *Journal of the American Medical Association*.

Even when no sexting occurs, online dating can be awkward and sometimes disturbing. Communication mostly through digital messages ignores factors such as body language, facial expressions, and vocal tones. All of these make face-to-face communication clearer, richer, and overall healthier than the online variety. Still, whatever its shortcomings, online dating is both pervasive and here to stay. So it is up to teens, with the help of trusted adults, to learn to use the new technology in responsible and healthy ways.

In whatever manner modern teens meet, interact, socialize, and date, connecting in one way or another with fellow teens is crucial. For the vast majority of them, high school is their first major exposure to society and the wider world they will occupy as adults. Therefore, it is essential that these relationships be as positive and rewarding as possible.

CHAPTER THREE

Healthy and Unhealthy Body Image

Teens who have a healthy body image tend to think positively about their bodies. They tend to be comfortable with their looks and have confidence in themselves. They most often maintain this healthy self-image by eating normal amounts of healthy foods, exercising regularly, getting plenty of sleep, and hanging out with friends who also have good body image and high self-esteem. Together, these factors form a sort of positive support system. With only occasional exceptions, young people with a healthy body image have a better chance of achieving happiness than those with a poor body image.

Teens with a poor body image tend to be displeased with how they look, which negatively affects their self-esteem. These young people tend to spend a lot of time thinking about how other people view them. They might be concerned about whether they are too fat or too thin, whether their hair is too curly or too straight, or whether they are too short or too tall.

Obsessing over one's body image can result in a lot of anxiety. That anxiety is often magnified by all of the images people see around them—images of supermodels, actors, and athletes. These are people who, society says, represent the height of beauty and fitness. Constantly comparing oneself to these individuals can lead a person to question his or her own looks. And usually that person will come up short. Teens who do this often are more likely to develop an unhealthy body image. According to Northeastern University psychotherapist Amy Morin, "Movies, commercials, magazines, and websites portray beautiful people as ideal. Underweight models and photo-shopped images of perfection are everywhere. Diet products and beauty items send the message that being thinner and more attractive is the key to happiness and success."[31]

Some Consequences of Poor Body Image

In these and similar ways, society as a whole regularly puts pressure on teens to look, and sometimes act, certain ways. This can have serious consequences, in part because some people are naturally heavier or thinner or taller or shorter than average. Also, a small but ever-present number of people have one or another physical differences or disabilities. These can include spinal and other bone abnormalities, muscular problems such as muscular dystrophy, skin conditions like eczema, and various birth defects.

Many teens do not care about such differences in others, and they try to treat everyone with respect. But poor body image comes not from how others view your body. It comes from how *you* see it. Thus, a number of teens feel uncomfortable or even distressed about their looks, often to the confusion of their friends and classmates. California high school student Samantha Phan, for example, recalls that in seventh grade she was friends with a girl who constantly worried about how she looked:

> "Diet products and beauty items send the message that being thinner and more attractive is the key to happiness and success."[31]
>
> —Northeastern University psychotherapist Amy Morin

I never understood why; she was beautiful and, in fact, in much better shape than many of the other girls at school. She said she needed to get healthier. Soon, at lunch we would all sit and eat what we had packed—whether it be a sandwich, or leftovers from the night before. We all noticed that every day for the past week, the girl had only a small Chewy Granola bar for lunch. Later I found out what she meant by "healthier" was in fact skinnier. Which, may I add, is not the same. She began to look more tired and drained each day.[32]

Phan's friend, who suffered from poor body image, became abnormally thin for a while but eventually managed to return to a healthier weight. In some cases poor body image can lead to more serious consequences. One consists of bouts of depression, in which a teen feels overly sad and even unhappy with life in general. Of these individuals, some simply suffer in silence, while

Glorified images of supermodels, actors, and athletes with perfect hair, skin, and body types are everywhere. These images can negatively influence teen attitudes about their own bodies.

others resort to various forms of self-injury. The experts at the Palo Alto Medical Foundation explain:

Some teens may carve, scratch, or cut on their wrists, arms, or other parts of the body. It seems irrational to others, but when people are clinically depressed, it can seem like a way to let out the tension or pain. . . . Although self-injury and self-mutilation may give the recipient temporary relief, they are neither safe nor permanent solutions. It is important to get help from a health care professional as soon as possible.[33]

Three Primary Stages of Food Abuse

Although depression and self-harm are fairly common consequences of poor body image among teens, a far more prevalent reaction is to develop an eating disorder. Eating disorders are medical conditions that involve harmful eating habits and patterns. Usually those affected eat either too much or too little for a lengthy period of time and thereby suffer from various physical, emotional, and even social problems. One of the country's leading authorities on the subject—the National Eating Disorders Association (NEDA)—points out that eating disorders "are real, complex, and devastating conditions that can have serious consequences for health, productivity, and relationships. They are not a fad, phase or lifestyle choice. Eating disorders are serious, potentially life-threatening conditions that affect a person's emotional and physical health."[34]

Experts on eating disorders say that although poor body image is a major cause of these conditions, a related factor—low

"[When overwhelmed by feelings of anger and depression], some teens may carve, scratch, or cut on their wrists, arms, or other parts of the body."[33]

—California's Palo Alto Medical Foundation

Eating Disorders Among Young Men

For a long time, the common belief has been that eating disorders only affect young women. However, fairly large numbers of young men also get eating disorders. The Center for Eating Disorders, a facility in Maryland that treats these afflictions, explains why teenage males are also at risk for suffering from these disorders:

> As is the case with females, body image concerns appear to be one of the strongest variables in predicting eating disorders in males. Studies have demonstrated that the drive for thinness was a more important predictor of weight loss behaviors than psychological and/or family variables, and this desire was true of both adolescent males and females. Studies also demonstrate that cultural and media pressures on men for the "ideal body" are on the rise. While social and media pressures for female bodies often focus on being skinnier and thinner, the messages aimed at males often promote hyper-masculine bodies that are toned, muscular and perfectly groomed. Men are increasingly the target of diet and weight-loss advertisements, grooming/beauty products, cosmetic surgeries and the fashion industry which may be contributing to rising rates of body dissatisfaction among males.

Center for Eating Disorders, "Males & Eating Disorders: Breaking Through Stigma and Stereotypes," 2015. www.eatingdisorder.org.

self-esteem—is often also involved, especially in teens. Low self-esteem often leads to other negative feelings, which compound one another. It is common, for instance, for a sufferer to view her- or himself as not only physically unattractive, but also unintelligent, untalented, and/or worthless. The person may feel inadequate to accomplish average tasks and navigate social situations that other teens appear to handle easily and well. Upset by what he or she sees as a failing, the affected teen may try to cope by abusing food in some way in hopes of feeling better, at least temporarily.

Doctors and other health experts recognize three principal eating disorders: binge eating disorder (also called compulsive overeating), bulimia, and anorexia. Each has typical, recognizable symptoms, or signs and patterns of behavior, that distinguish it from other illnesses. Nevertheless, the three disorders are closely related. All three involve the misuse of food, resulting in often harmful physical effects. Also, each is part of, or a stage in, a larger pattern of food abuse, and one typically leads to another in a disturbing progression, or continuum. For instance, bulimics and anorexics almost always start out as binge eaters. Not all binge eaters go on to become bulimics, but some do; similarly, not all bulimics go on to become anorexics, but some do.

Feeling Worthless and Broken

The most common eating disorder in the country, binge eating involves repeated episodes of consuming unusually large amounts of food. The food can be of any kind, but usually it is highly caloric and fattening. Characteristic fare for a binger includes pie, cake, cookies, doughnuts, ice cream, potato chips, and other snack

Frequent late-night binges can lead to weight gain and feelings of shame. Teens who binge often find themselves ensnared in a frustrating cycle of repeated bingeing, weight gain, and dieting.

foods. Healthy eaters frequently express amazement at how much of these types of food a teenage binger can pack away. Typical is eating an entire pie and a half gallon of ice cream in only fifteen minutes, followed by still more bingeing. Even a moderate binge eater usually consumes four thousand or five thousand calories in one twenty- to thirty-minute binge, about as much food as an average person eats in two full days.

Furthermore, a teen with this disorder engages in four to seven binges a week; meanwhile, a young person with a severe case may do it eight to fourteen times per week. Most often teen binge eaters experience a loss of control while bingeing, as well as feelings of shame, regret, distress, and guilt afterward. Because of the guilt, she or he may manage to stop bingeing for a week or two but always returns to the old pattern sooner or later. It is also common for a bingeing teen to gain some weight. That may prompt her or him to go on a diet. However, that approach is also typically doomed to failure and can lead to a cycle of repeated bingeing, weight gain, and dieting.

Making matters worse, the cycles of bingeing and dieting can and often do reinforce an overriding cycle of depression and bingeing. That is, frequently a teen begins bingeing because she or he is depressed, and the bingeing then causes more depression. And it is not unusual for a depressed person to feel worthless, broken, and beyond repair. A Colorado teenage binger named Jennifer recalls such feelings, saying, "I always felt so much bigger than the lean teens I went to school with, and it seemed they could eat anything they wanted. It was so unfair. Why couldn't I do that? I was told it would catch up with them, but that never felt like much consolation. That also contributed to feeling like there's something inherently wrong with me, that I was broken."[35]

Trying to Get Rid of the Food

Jennifer's battle with binge eating disorder never developed further than her seemingly endless cycle of bingeing and dieting. She did not progress further along the eating disorders continuum and become bulimic. Bulimics are, in essence, bingers who deliberately purge, or vomit up, most of what they have just eaten. (Some bulimics alternately get rid of the food by using laxatives and/or diuretics, medications that make them go to the bathroom.)

Such a purge is a desperate attempt to reverse one's last binge. But that attempt always fails, in part because a bulimic will binge again. Also, following an inevitable pattern, a bulimic will purge again, despite experiencing a number of harmful physical side effects of frequent purging. One of those side effects is swelling of the esophagus—the tube leading from the back of the throat to the stomach. A second, related side effect consists of small gashes in the lining of the mouth or throat. "The summer after I graduated high school," teen bulimic Krista Barlow later recollected, "I noticed I had a lot of blood coming from my throat when I spit. I noticed it more when I brushed my teeth. I knew I needed to stop because I had damaged my esophagus badly."[36] In addition, teenagers and other young people suffering from bulimia tend to become dehydrated, or lacking in fluids, and their constant purging can cause imbalances in vital minerals their bodies need.

> "I knew I needed to stop because I had damaged my esophagus badly."[36]
>
> —Teenaged bulimic Krista Barlow

According to the National Eating Disorders Information Centre, teen bulimics binge and purge from one to three or more times per week. Like Barlow, they tend to do it in secret, carefully trying to hide the behavior from family and friends. Often, however, someone finds out because several of symptoms of the disease are difficult to conceal. Another national organization that deals with abusive eating, Eating Disorders Hope, says that a telltale sign to watch for in a teen is when she or he frequently disappears into the bathroom during or after a meal. Also, a sufferer may engage in odd rituals that involve food; for example, stealing or hoarding it. Other signs of the disorder include fatigue, sore

Eating Disorders: Treatment vs. Cure

Experts on eating disorders all agree that these ailments can be treated using a number of methods. They caution, however, that even the most successful treatment cannot totally defeat eating disorders because to date, science has found no complete cure for them. Instead, the best a sufferer can expect is to learn to manage the disorder in such a way that it no longer disrupts her or his life.

Treatment for these conditions consists first of trying to physically repair and heal a body that has been damaged by months or years of bingeing and purging, yo-yo dieting, and/or starvation. Another general approach to treatment is the attempt, through professional counseling, to heal the mental and emotional scars the patient has acquired while suffering from an eating disorder. Often those who are helping the patient get better employ forms of both, either in one-on-one or group counseling sessions. Meanwhile, the most severe cases of anorexia are most often treated in a hospital, where a sufferer can receive professional care around the clock.

throat, dizziness, tremors, muscle cramps, blurred vision, indigestion, constipation, nausea, and diarrhea. Being obsessed with body image and weight and displaying frequent mood swings are also possible signs of bulimia.

A Destructive Cycle

Many teenaged bulimics continue their destructive cycle of bingeing and purging well into their twenties and even beyond. A few, however, escalate the behavior while still teens and progress to the last and potentially most dangerous condition on the eating disorders continuum. In effect, they cross over the line from bulimia into anorexia.

Anorexia is mainly associated with abnormal thinness. So many people are surprised to learn that the vast majority of anorexics start out as binge eaters and have problems with excess weight. For an undetermined length of time, most often fairly short, a future anorexic will binge and purge and at intervals gain a few pounds. However, she or he will eventually develop an intense fear of becoming fat. Suddenly, the person decides the only

One way to overcome negative body image is to try new activities. A new exercise class or cooking healthy meals with a friend can result in positive changes, both physical and mental.

way to avoid that fate is to reject food whenever possible, and a cycle of self-starvation begins.

Typically, an anorexic teen will eat only foods that have very few calories per serving—such as lettuce, carrots, and apples. She or he will become obsessed with avoiding weight gain. Even when that individual's body looks far too thin and malnourished in the eyes of others, he or she will continue to restrict food.

In part this is because anorexics no longer have the ability to see their body in a healthy, rationale manner. The poor body image that contributed to developing an eating disorder in the first place now intensifies into something even worse; medical professionals call it body dysmorphic disorder. According to the National Association of Anorexia Nervosa and Associated Disorders (ANAD), this disorder "is characterized as an obsession with an imaginary defect in physical appearance or an extreme concern with a slight physical blemish, which other individuals may not even recognize."[37] For an anorexic, the "imaginary defect" is a fat body, and he or she will imagine being fat even after becoming abnormally skinny.

Not surprisingly, anorexics can no longer make good decisions for themselves. At this point, they face a real threat to both life and happiness. A teen named Julie Saunders wrote about her ordeal with anorexia, saying,

> "I cried when I thought of food and berated myself for eating. I was a shell of who I once was."[38]
>
> —Teenaged anorexic Julie Saunders

My hair fell out, I was always dizzy, my clothes didn't fit me. My eyes were dark holes. I cried when I thought of food and berated myself for eating. I was a shell of who I once was. Every day I thought to myself that I couldn't live this way forever but the alternative was me gaining weight, and at the time, that was even worse than being consumed by the monster inside me that was my eating disorder.[38]

Some Bad News and Some Good News

Saunders's bout with anorexia was not unusual; many American teens find themselves somewhere on the eating disorders continuum. In fact, the bad news for teens is that most Americans with eating disorders first acquire them in the teen years. ANAD estimates that a whopping 82 percent of Americans with eating disorders developed them by age twenty. That means that teens have a major risk factor for suffering from those ailments. That is not surprising, experts say, considering that poor body image is so prevalent among teens.

In contrast, the good news for teens is that, although eating disorders are not completely curable, they *are* treatable. Furthermore, even someone with a serious case of anorexia can recover from that condition's worst effects and lead a mostly normal life. Eating Disorders Hope, NEDA, ANAD, and other such organizations all concur that teens and others struggling with eating disorders should seek professional help. "There is always hope for recovery," NEDA adds. Negative feelings associated with disordered eating "may reappear during times of stress, but there are many good techniques individuals with eating disorders can learn to help manage their emotions and keep behaviors from returning."[39]

Those techniques can even help such a person learn to have a healthy body image again. They are all about exposing oneself only to positive imagery. According to a spokesperson for the Palo Alto Medical Foundation, "Instead of surrounding yourself with images and talk of negative body image, use that time to try a new exercise class or cook a healthy meal with a friend. By spending more time doing the healthy, fun activities you love and less time obsessing over your body, you are well on your way to having a healthier body image."[40]

CHAPTER FOUR

Major Life Transitions

When American middle school student Cody Burger was fourteen, his life changed forever. His father contracted cancer and died a few months later. "I was living through something that most teenagers don't experience," Cody later recalled. "And I had to figure out how to be a kid after losing my father."[41]

The death of a parent, sibling, other relative, or close friend is one of the major life transitions that some teens experience. Another is moving to a new town, state, or country, forcing a teen to suddenly adjust to a new school, new friends, or even a new language and culture. Other transitions include the divorce or separation of one's parents; an abrupt financial loss or gain in the teen's family, often necessitating a different lifestyle; a teen's serious questioning of his or her long-held faith or spirituality; and coming out, or admitting to family, friends, and others that one is gay. Even graduating from high school and going off to college or getting a full-time job can be a major life transition.

> "Like adults, teens experience stress due to significant life changes."[42]
>
> —Mental health therapist Kathleen Smith

One thing that these and other life transitions have in common is that they may, and usually do, cause teens to feel various levels of stress, confusion, anxiety, and apprehension about what the future may hold for them. Indeed, says mental health therapist Kathleen Smith, "Like adults, teens experience stress due to significant life changes," and "not knowing how to cope with big changes is overwhelming and can be confusing for the developing teen."[42]

Adjusting to a New Town and School

Teenagers' reactions to these life transitions can vary considerably. Much can depend on their individual personality and how much support they receive from family and friends. Some teens are fortunate enough to have both the outside support and inner strength to deal with a change with a minimal amount of disruption or distress. They may be temporarily flustered or confused by the sudden change but still manage to take it in stride and adjust fairly easily to the new situation.

This is how Priya Kshirsagar, who attended grade school and middle school in Ohio, was able to avoid most of the potential emotional upset during her first major life transition: a cross-country move. She later wrote:

> On my first day of high school, I found myself torn from my childhood in the Ohio suburbs and in the middle of a huge school right in sunny California. I was in a sea of people, and all I could think as I stood in the lines for registration was how lost I felt. As I looked around, I wondered who could be my friend. . . . I found myself thinking a great deal about what to say, and how to act. Finally, after meeting some people at sports practices and classes, I relaxed and found myself acting without unnecessary thought and stress. I soon formed close friends and felt like I finally had a place in my new home.[43]

Trouble Adjusting to Change

In contrast, a young person may experience a good deal more difficulty in dealing with a particular life transition. She or he may struggle to cope with such a major change and may feel overwhelmed by the stress. In such a case, his or her reaction may be to experience anxiety, become depressed, have trouble sleeping, or abuse drugs or alcohol.

Frequently, when a teen's reaction to a life transition is of this more challenging kind, therapists and other experts will diagnose

Moving to a new city and school can be challenging. Walking on campus for the first time, knowing no one and seeing groups of students talking and laughing, can be a lonely and uncomfortable feeling.

her or him as having an adjustment disorder. An adjustment disorder is an emotional or behavioral reaction to a stressful event or change in a person's life. According to Georgia psychotherapist Drew Adelman:

> A diagnosis of adjustment disorder can occur when a major life stress or change disrupts normal coping mechanisms and makes it difficult or impossible for a person to cope with new circumstances. Symptoms of an adjustment disorder begin within three months of a life transition and often include a depressed or anxious mood, changes in daily habits, feelings of overwhelming stress and panic, difficulty enjoying activities, and changes in sleeping or eating. This condition may also lead an individual to engage in reckless or dangerous behavior, avoid family and friends, or even have thoughts of suicide.[44]

When Parents Divorce: Tips from a Fellow Teen

Leigha Winters, a teenager in her first year of college, remembers her parents' divorce vividly and offers the following advice to younger teens going through that major life transition:

> Divorce is a tremendous time of change in your family that can bring out a lot of emotions inside you. Some teens experience feelings of anger, guilt, or sadness about their parents divorcing. They might feel like they are somehow to blame for their parents breaking up. It is important to remember that you are not to blame. . . . You may experience a variety of emotions for each difficult change that accompanies a divorce. Some of these changes may initially include having two households instead of one, observing conflict between your parents, having to switch schools, enduring the court and legal process, and not seeing both parents every day. . . . But remember that things will settle down and it gets easier. However, if you find you are having trouble adjusting to your new life after your parents' divorce, consider speaking with your physician. He or she can help you find a professional counselor to help you deal with your feelings.

Leigha Winters, "Divorce," Palo Alto Medical Foundation, 2015. www.pamf.org.

New York native Ivana Silverio is a teen whose family relocation caused her to develop an adjustment disorder. She had just finished her junior year of high school when her parents informed her they were moving to the Dominican Republic. The young woman had to instantly try to adjust not only to a different town and school, but also to a completely different culture. She remembers feeling totally uprooted, fearful, and hopeless. "You experience a lot of mental battles at once," she explains. "I can feel sick one day and happy the next, or depressed in the morning and by noon I'm out to take on the world again."[45]

In fact, Silverio never fully adjusted to the big move in her remaining teen years. Only after going to college and taking up long-distance running as a hobby did she leave behind all the stresses her family's move had thrust on her. "For me," she says, "running was more mental than physical. Crossing the finish line was like crossing the mental thresholds trying to hold me back."[46]

Divorce: Family Life Altered Forever

Another kind of life transition that many teens have considerable difficulty adjusting to is the divorce of their parents. Divorce, and often the events leading toward it, can be extremely painful and confusing for young people. The emotional toll is long lasting. "For adolescents, parental divorce is usually a formative and watershed event," says Texas psychologist Carl E. Pickhardt. "Family life is altered forever after."[47]

With few exceptions, parental divorce is a central change in a teen's life that automatically sets in motion several smaller yet still life-altering changes. Sometimes, she or he has to change schools and may even have to move to a new town or state. Also, that young person must learn to adjust to spending time with each parent separately, and that can be extra stressful if the mother and father now resent each other. Or a teen might end up living full time with only one parent because a judge ruled it must be that way. Making matters worse, often neither parent can now afford to give the teen the material comforts she or he was formerly accustomed to.

> "For adolescents, parental divorce is usually a formative and watershed event."[47]
>
> —Texas psychologist Carl E. Pickhardt

In addition, Pickhardt points out, for a teenager, "divorce often results in some loss of trust in, and respect for, the leadership of parents." The teen does not necessarily stop loving the parents. "However, in adolescent eyes, through divorce parents have put adult self-interest above the interests of children and family. In response, the teenager tends to become more detached from parents."[48]

Whatever the immediate effects of the divorce, such changes in the family can cause a lot of confusion, anger, and stress for a teenager. Seventeen-year-old Creigh recollects what he went through when his parents divorced:

> It was an abrupt transition. One day I was living among the piles of boxes at my house, and the next I was sleeping on a mattress on the ground in a foreign house, going to a completely different bus stop in a different neighborhood. My 17th birthday [party took place] only a matter of months after the divorce, and it was a nightmare. Both of my parents were there, along with most of the family on my mom's side. Everyone tried to pretend that everything was normal, but it wasn't. Some of my relatives wouldn't even come, just because my dad was there. The tension was almost unbearable.[49]

When parents divorce, young people experience a range of feelings. One teen found journaling to be a helpful way to manage the stress he felt in connection with the changes taking place in his family.

Over time, Creigh, recalls, he learned to cope with the changes his parents' divorce had brought about. "I'm grateful that I at least used the positive coping mechanism of keeping a journal about my experience, which I think really helped me manage stress. My journal kept me sane." Creigh also began sharing his feelings with others. This proved to be another important way of coping with the hurt and uncertainty of his parents' broken marriage, as he explains:

It was only in the second year after the divorce that I started talking about the impact of the divorce on me, and I've just recently stopped censoring what I tell my friends. Even private people like me need a support system, though, and since you can't grow one overnight, I ended up seeing a therapist. I can honestly say that it helped a lot and I wish I had made the decision to see one earlier.[50]

Dealing with Grief

Mental health experts generally agree with Creigh's point about therapy—that when possible, teens undergoing serious and stressful life changes should seek some sort of professional counseling. Yet not all teens who suffer from such stress choose that approach. This was what happened with Cody Burger after his father passed away from cancer when the young man was just fourteen. Cody insisted on dealing with his grief in his own way. This may have been partly because he knew in advance that his dad was going to die.

Unlike Cody's experience, for many teens the need to grieve the death of a parent or other loved one frequently comes suddenly. The death might be the result of a heart attack, a car accident, or a suicide, which all are unexpected. A surviving teen typically has never had to deal with death up close before and has no idea how to approach the grieving process. So he or she may reflexively look to adult authority figures, including therapists, for guidance.

In contrast, Cody had a few months to prepare for his father's death and therefore may have been able to mentally prepare for it to some degree. As a result, only a few days after the funeral, he returned to school. "School felt like a safe haven," he recalls. "Yes, people expressed their sympathies, and I was thankful for their show of support. But at the same time, I didn't want to hear anything about my dad; I wanted school to be unchanged. I needed to complete assignments and make up tests, and the routine felt normal and comfortable. In fact, school kept me sane through my grieving process."[51]

Another reason that Cody chose to work out his grief by trying to return to a state of normalcy was that he believed he needed to step up and to some degree fill his father's shoes. This feeling is quite common among male teens grieving a lost parent, experts say. According to Alan D. Wolfelt, founder of the Center for Loss and Life Transition, in Boulder, Colorado, they often feel that they are "expected to be 'grown up' and support other members of the family, particularly a surviving parent and/or younger brothers and sisters. Many teens have been told, 'Now, you will have to take care of your family.'"[52] Cody himself echoed this sentiment, saying, "I had to grow up and be more mature than I was. I didn't have a choice, as I had to help make things better for my family."[53]

Still another reason that Cody did not seek adult guidance was that he was unaware that such help was available in his town. Many communities offer a variety of services for teens who are experiencing loss and grief. Help can be found through school counselors, trusted adults, religious organizations, and private counseling.

Turning His World Around

Life transitions come in many forms, and although not all of these transitions involve loss or grief, they can be just as challenging. When an LGBT teen comes out to family and friends, this is also

Teens who are experiencing grief and anxiety do not need to struggle alone with their feelings. Many counseling options exist—through schools, communities, medical clinics, and religious organizations.

a major life transition. "It was the moment that I had been waiting for my whole entire life," says sixteen-year-old Jordy. "Saying the words, 'I am gay,' turned my world completely around."[54] He is not alone. Although fear of rejection, harassment, and violence still exist, many LGBT youth are revealing themselves to the people who matter most to them. A major 2018 Human Rights Campaign study of LGBT youth found that more than 60 percent come out in their teen years to selected family and friends.

Despite their fears, LGBT young people are coming out because they do not want to constantly live a lie and conceal their true selves. Dana Buzzelli, who came out when she was sixteen, expresses a typical point of view. "To me," she says, "coming out

Crushed by Her Father's Passing

In an online article, a young woman named Annie Walters describes her reaction to her father's death when she was just fourteen years old:

> I would plaster on a fake smile, go out with friends and continue to go to school like I was fine. On the inside, however, I was crushed under the weight of my depression and constant numbness. Things that used to give me pleasure were now tasks that took what little energy I had away from me; I stopped writing and had to force myself to go out with friends to "keep up with appearances." I stopped eating and lost weight. Once again, I had to force myself to eat to keep everyone around me from thinking that there was something wrong. By the year anniversary of my dad's death, I couldn't take the depression any longer. I could no longer recognize the girl in the mirror; a once happy, full of life girl was now paled by grief and sadness.

> Eventually, Annie began seeing a therapist. She now calls therapy "one of the best things to come out of my grief and depression" and adds, "I've learned how to express my emotions, instead of keeping them bottled up."

Annie Walters, "After My Father Died," *Hello Grief* (blog), 2010. www.hellogrief.org.

was all about being true to myself. I totally rejected the idea that I should hide how I felt, as if it was wrong or horrible. I also wasn't comfortable with lying about who I was or who I loved."[55] Jordy's decision to come out was also guided by a desire to be true to himself—and to be accepted for who he is. "All I wanted was to be treated normally,"[56] he states.

Teens describe mixed reactions to their coming out. Some friends, relatives, and acquaintances were supportive—others less so. Sixteen-year-old Indiana teen Kiara was fortunate enough to receive largely positive reactions. "My dad's truly really accepting," she says. "My mom didn't take it well at first, but I feel like she's getting more used to it now. People at school, they don't care and it doesn't bother them much."[57] In contrast, when a teenager named Erin came out to her mother, the latter refused to accept it. Erin's mother said it must be a temporary phase that Erin would eventually work through.

The difference between these two scenarios is that the parent was supportive in one but not in the other. In the long run, the support of parents and/or close friends can help a teen get through this and other key life transitions. "Your life is changing, just like your body," says a teen participating in Palo Alto Medical Foundation's Summer Wellness Programs. "As you grow older you will develop the skills you need to manage stress, but for now, just remember you are in a tough spot and need all the support you can get. Reach out to adults and friends—there is always someone there who cares for you."[58]

CHAPTER FIVE

Signs of Trouble

School pressures, obsessing over one's looks, worries about friends, and experiencing significant life transitions can all cause even well-adjusted teens to feel stressed-out. That sort of stress is a normal part of growing up. It tends to be temporary, and most young people learn to weather it and move on. Overall, their mental health remains stable. In fact, a person's ability "to cope with the normal stresses of life"[59] and remain productive is the very definition of *mental health*, according to the World Health Organization.

Not every teen has the ability to adapt to and overcome the pressures of everyday life. Sometimes, everyday life brings challenges that go beyond the norm. Some teens experience more physical or emotional setbacks than others do, are more emotionally vulnerable than average, or may lack the strong support from family and friends that others enjoy. These adolescents are less able to cope with and recover from the setbacks and manage the stress, and as a result they are more debilitated by both. In turn, their inability to cope can trigger negative, harmful emotions and behaviors, such as depression and substance abuse. According to the National Institutes of Health (NIH), some 20 percent of all teens ages thirteen to eighteen will experience such a mental health problem. Because the thinking and actions of these teens are at least temporarily disordered, medical experts often call some of those problems "mental disorders."

Studies by the CDC and other leading health organizations indicate that, besides eating disorders, the most commonly diagnosed emotional problems among today's teens are anxiety, depression, and attention-deficit/hyperactivity disorder (ADHD).

According to the CDC, by age seventeen about 7 percent of teens will be diagnosed with anxiety disorder, more than 3 percent will suffer from prolonged depression, and over 9 percent will have ADHD. In addition, the Pew Research Center says, more than 6 percent will try to compensate for emotional setbacks and stress by using illegal drugs.

Accurately identifying these problems in teenagers can often be difficult or uncertain. This is because it is fairly common for teens to sometimes feel anxious or depressed and to experiment with drugs and other potentially harmful substances. But experts point out that the signs of real trouble are when these feelings and activities are repetitive and severe. As a researcher at the NIH phrases it, "Such normal behaviors can be distinguished from more serious problems by the duration, persistence, and impact of the symptoms."[60]

When Anxiety Becomes Worrisome

How factors like persistence and severity can transform a fairly normal situation into a troubling one is well illustrated by the way anxiety affects some teens. Everyone, including large numbers of teens, experiences some degree of anxiety from time to time. Middle school and high school students frequently feel anxious before a big exam, for example, or before opening night of a school play. In contrast, says Dr. Todd Callahan of Boston Children's Hospital, "An anxiety disorder is when your anxiety becomes so great that you feel very scared or uneasy in situations that are not dangerous. Increased anxiety can cause you to avoid certain activities or perform poorly at school. It can even make you feel physically sick. If these feelings are frequent and have lasted for weeks or months, you may have an anxiety disorder."[61]

"Increased anxiety can cause you to avoid certain activities or perform poorly at school."[61]

—Dr. Todd Callahan, Boston Children's Hospital

Two of the symptoms of this more serious type of anxiety are trouble falling asleep and frequent headaches. Others can include trouble concentrating, irritability or crankiness, quick heartbeat, increased sweating, tingling in the hands, and the inability to let go of a particular worry or thought. Again, individually and for short periods, none of these is necessarily unusual. But if someone experiences two or more of them consistently for weeks or months, the symptoms may be signs of something worrisome.

They may, for instance, signal that the person has perhaps the most common form of anxiety in teens. Callahan and other experts call it social anxiety disorder, or social phobia. It is typical for a sufferer to be constantly worried about what others think about her or him or what they might say. The person is overly concerned about standing out in a crowd or saying something weird or em-

Feeling anxious before a big exam is not unusual. When that anxiety does not fade, or when it causes a person to avoid activities or become physically sick, this is a sign of something that might require professional help.

barrassing and does not want to be the center of attention. It is common for him or her to avoid raising a hand in class and to fear participating in any group activity with classmates. Moreover, a teen with social anxiety disorder may stay away from school altogether whenever possible, as well as develop eating problems or feel depressed. A high school senior named Alicia Tatar recalls that when she was in the seventh grade, she was

> in the nurse's office every week and missing a few days of school each month. I was anxious outside of school, too. I'd started taking dance classes, but I'd skip them or make excuses to stay home. . . . It was around this time that I started to become depressed. I stopped eating because I had no appetite. . . . Eighth grade was even harder. I missed an impressive amount of school and even more social opportunities. I almost failed gym because I was too anxious to change and participate. . . . I felt helpless and hopeless.[62]

Fortunately for Alicia, she found out that anxiety disorders are treatable and sought and received help. First, she went to a therapist for one-on-one sessions in which they talked about the possible causes of her anxiety. Therapists also sometimes recommend that teens join group sessions with people their own age. For the most severe cases, therapists can refer a teen to a doctor, who may prescribe medications. Furthermore, therapists often advise teenage anxiety patients to get involved in activities that will help them relax, such as listening to peaceful music, going for long walks, or doing yoga.

Clinical Depression

Alicia reported that one of the several troubling aspects of her anxiety disorder was feeling like she should avoid food. Her therapist told her she had become borderline anorexic. This shows that one mental disorder can contribute to or trigger another.

A Teen Describes Her Bout with Anxiety

In 2018 eighteen-year-old Grace Griffin, who had recently graduated from Portsmouth High School in New Hampshire, published a book about her years-long struggle with social anxiety disorder. The work tells how for a long time she was terrified to be called on in class. Typically, she candidly tells an interviewer, she ate lunch alone, in an empty classroom or a stall in one of the school bathrooms. Describing the crippling anxiety that ruled her life, she explains that it got so bad that she did not "want to wake up every day because the thought of having to go to school and see people and talk in front of people sounded horrible." Eventually, a fellow student took an interest in her plight. That mentor dragged her to the lunchroom and made her sit and eat with others, and over time that helped. Griffin says that these "lunchers," as she calls them, eventually became her best buddies. She steadily improved emotionally and in her senior year began writing the book. Her goal in doing it was to aid others as well as herself. "I just thought to try and help at least one person by telling how I felt," she says.

Quoted in Hadley Barndollar, "NH Teen Authors Book About 'Surviving High School with Social Anxiety Disorder,'" *Bangor (ME) Daily News*, August 13, 2018. https://bangordailynews.com.

Similarly, Alicia attested that she sometimes felt depressed. Not only can depression be a symptom of extreme anxiety, but severe depression is a disorder in and of itself. Medical experts call that more severe problem *clinical depression* to differentiate it from the normal version in which someone temporarily feels sad or gloomy. Usually, a person who is clinically depressed is overwhelmed by feelings of hopelessness and may come to see life in general as no longer worth living.

A number of different factors can contribute to depression. Medical studies indicate that one of them is having too little or too much of some specific brain chemicals. Family history can also be a factor because your risk of developing clinical depression is a good deal higher if one or more of your relatives have had it. Other factors that can contribute are sad or tragic life events, such as child abuse, traumatic divorce, and the sudden death of a friend or relative.

Although these factors may seem fairly obvious and clear-cut, clinical depression is often difficult to diagnose in teens. This is

because adults traditionally expect teens to act moody sometimes and to be extremely sad when first forced to deal with death
and other emotional traumas. Another problem is simple lack of
knowledge. Both adolescents and their parents, and their teachers as well, frequently are not aware that certain emotions and
actions can be symptoms of depression when they happen in
clusters or last for more than a few weeks.

Those telltale symptoms may include expressions of extreme
sadness and hopelessness, as well as a lack of enthusiasm, energy, or motivation. The young person may also start performing
poorly in school, withdraw from sports or other extracurricular activities, and undergo fairly abrupt changes in eating and
sleeping patterns. Among the other common symptoms of depression are periodic outbursts of anger for no apparent reason,

Grief is a normal reaction to the death of a close friend or
relative. The sadness of loss might initially overwhelm other
aspects of daily life, but if that continues or worsens over time, a
visit with a doctor or other health professional might be in order.

overreacting to simple criticism, frequent forgetfulness, poor self-esteem, and abusing alcohol or drugs. Teens may also "become sexually promiscuous to avoid feelings of depression," the health advocacy organization Mental Health America points out. Or they "may express their depression through hostile, aggressive, risk-taking behavior. But such behaviors only lead to new problems, deeper levels of depression, and destroyed relationships with friends, family, law enforcement, or school officials."[63]

Diagnosing and Treating Depression

A teenager named Topanga Brown experienced many of these symptoms and behaviors yet went for a long time before being diagnosed with clinical depression. Beginning at age fifteen, she recalls,

> my school work began to plummet and I stopped being the social butterfly I once was. I would go to the bathroom at school and [feel panicky and cry]. I would not return until the next class had begun. Neither my friends, nor my teachers confronted me about withdrawing from my usual activities, which made me feel even more isolated. I felt like they didn't care that I was barely speaking or doing any of the homework I once loved to do.[64]

As it turned out, one person did care about Brown's troubling behavior—her older sister, who fortunately had had some training in recognizing the signs of depression. The sister took Brown to a medical specialist, who officially diagnosed the condition and began treating it.

Similarly, one young man, who prefers not to give his name, recognized the symptoms of clinical depression in himself. At

Gay Teens Are More Likely to Consider Suicide

Gay teens who are in the closet—that is, who hide their sexual orientation from most people they know—are at a significantly higher risk for attempting suicide. This was a key finding of a 2018 study published in the *American Journal of Preventive Medicine*. The researchers surveyed almost seven thousand high school students from across the country, asking questions about various risky behaviors. Approximately 32 percent of the students who admitted to being gay also said that they routinely hid their sexual orientation from most people they knew. An alarming 46 percent of those same gay teens said they had either attempted or thought about attempting suicide in the past year. In contrast, only 22 percent of the other teenage respondents said that they had had suicidal thoughts or behaviors. These findings are important, says West Virginia University medical researcher John Blosnich. Suicide "has been the tenth leading cause of death in the general U.S. population for at least a decade," he explains, "and the third leading cause of death among teenagers. You can imagine that a huge concern for teenagers who experience conflict with their sexual identity is whether they will be rejected by their family and friends."

Quoted in Carolyn Crist, "Teens Who Hide Their Sexuality Have Higher Suicide Risk, Study Finds," HuffPost, March 21, 2018. www.huffingtonpost.com.

age eighteen he suspected he had the disorder. Later, in a post on a young men's health website, he explained that he had been feeling that way for three years. Moreover, "it got worse when my oldest brother died two years ago." He added, "I'm honestly tired of feeling like this and I want to change."[65] The therapy that teens with clinical depression typically receive can take different forms. But it always begins with counseling, which itself can vary in form. It can be one-on-one (patient and therapist), group (patient and a few peers), or family (patient and close relatives). The initial talks aim at finding out what triggered the illness. Also, a psychiatrist may prescribe various medications that will help the teen feel less sad or distraught. In addition, there may be

> "[My] school work began to plummet and I stopped being the social butterfly I once was."[64]
>
> —Topanga Brown, a teenager who suffered from clinical depression

longer-range therapy sessions that explore a teen's painful feelings and teach her or him various coping skills. Through therapy a teen also learns how to develop healthier relationships at home and at school.

Dealing with ADHD

Counseling and other forms of therapy are also available for ADHD, which affects boys more often than girls. Like depression, ADHD can run in families. A person with ADHD has more than average difficulty paying attention, may be restless and nearly constantly active, or may do something impulsively, without thinking it through. Callahan adds that ADHD is a spectrum disorder, which "means that some people have a little bit, some people have a medium amount, and some people have a lot of difficulty. Remember that people with ADHD are just as smart as other people. Some people think Albert Einstein had ADHD. In fact, people with ADHD are often very creative and adventurous."[66]

Max, a seventeen-year-old Massachusetts high school student, has ADHD. He regularly finds it hard to concentrate, as well as to focus on new tasks assigned to him, which negatively affects his schoolwork. "If something doesn't interest me, it's a titanic struggle for me to focus on it," he says. "The act of doing it is so unwelcome."[67] At one point, for example, he was assigned a research paper but kept putting it off. He finally began to work on it two days before it was due, but by then there was not enough time left and he did not finish it.

Max was disappointed to discover that no cure for ADHD currently exists. But he was happy that treatments are available that can help reduce the symptoms and allow the sufferer to function fairly normally. Certain medications can reduce the person's hyperactivity and help him or her more effectively focus, work, and learn. Meanwhile, counselors can teach the parents of a teen with ADHD how to help their child stay organized and stick to schedules.

Young people experiencing emotional difficulties should never be ashamed to ask for help. One-on-one counseling is just one option for helping teens overcome their troubles and learn ways to develop healthy relationships and positive self-image.

Illegal Substance Abuse

One thing that severe anxiety, clinical depression, and ADHD have in common is that a majority of people who have them first experienced them in their teens. The same can be said of drug abuse. According to the CDC, most adults with a drug addiction first experimented with those substances before they turned twenty-one, and the vast majority began while still in their teens.

Authorities at the CDC and other experts also caution that not all teens who decide to try illegal drugs become addicted to them. Many merely briefly experiment with them, just as they experiment with legal drugs like alcohol and nicotine (in tobacco). Studies show that the chief motives behind such experimentation are curiosity, peer pressure, stress, and a desire to momentarily escape life's daily grind.

Of the illegal drugs that teens most commonly use, by far the leading one is marijuana, or pot. In 2018, according to the Pew Research Center, about 22 percent of twelfth graders and 17 percent of tenth graders used pot at least once per month. In comparison, these percentages are roughly three times higher than that for teens' combined use of all other illegal drugs, including cocaine, heroin, meth, and ecstasy. One reason that medical experts increasingly consider pot separately from the others is that it is rapidly becoming more acceptable throughout society and is actually legal for adults in some states.

As for those teens who do use non-pot illegal drugs on a regular basis, the chances of getting hooked are high. For instance, a fifteen-year-old named Savannah became addicted to cocaine and pain pills, both of which she used daily. Finally, she says, one day she caught a glimpse of herself in a mirror and was startled at how much her appearance had deteriorated. "I nearly jumped out of my skin," she recalls. "I literally thought it was someone else in the bathroom with me. That's how bad it was, and I was terrified."[68] Shaken to the core, Savannah sought out a therapist, entered a treatment program, and got sober.

There is good news for other teens as well. Numerous studies indicate that the rate of teenage non-pot drug abuse has been declining in recent years. In 2019 the Pew Research Center announced that the proportion of teens regularly using those illicit substances fell from 10 percent in the mid-1990s to just 6 percent in 2018. Moreover, even those who become addicted can get treated and recover, as Savannah did.

Those fortunate teens will join the ranks of classmates who, like Topanga Brown, have recovered from various emotional disorders. What distinguishes Brown's case from many others is her personal commitment to keep other teens from suffering as she did. Although still healing from her bouts with depression, she says she has made it her "mission to help others, like my sister did for me. Even if I help only one person in my entire life fight this battle, it will be well worth it."[69]

SOURCE NOTES

Introduction: Stress Among Teens Is on the Rise

1. Quoted in TeensHealth, "What Stresses You Out About School?" https://kidshealth.org.
2. Juliana M. Horowitz and Nikki Graf, "Most U.S. Teens See Anxiety and Depression as a Major Problem Among Their Peers," Pew Research Center, February 20, 2019. www.pewsocialtrends.org.
3. Kathleen Smith, "6 Common Triggers of Teen Stress," PsyCom. www.psycom.net.
4. Katie Hurley, "Resilience in Children: Strategies to Strengthen Your Kids," PsyCom. www.psycom.net.
5. Horowitz and Graf, "Most U.S. Teens See Anxiety and Depression as a Major Problem Among Their Peers."

Chapter One: Balancing Home and School

6. Nancy Brown, "Life Balance," Palo Alto Medical Foundation, 2015. www.pamf.org.
7. Smith, "6 Common Triggers of Teen Stress."
8. Quoted in Patty Neighmond, "School Stress Takes a Toll on Health, Teens and Parents Say," NPR, December 2, 2013. www.npr.org.
9. Quoted in Alexandra Thurmond, "Under Pressure: Teens Speak Out About Stress," *Teen Vogue*, March 17, 2014. www.teenvogue.com.
10. Peg Streep, "The Enduring Pain of Childhood Verbal Abuse," *Tech Support* (blog), *Psychology Today*, November 14, 2016. www.psychologytoday.com.
11. Sargunjot Kaur, "Academic Pressure," Palo Alto Medical Foundation, 2013. www.pamf.org.
12. Quoted in Neighmond, "School Stress Takes a Toll on Health, Teens and Parents Say."

13. Quoted in Jeanne Goodes, "Tips for Helping Teens Balance School and Sport," Breaking Muscle. https://breakingmuscle.com.

14. Goodes, "Tips for Helping Teens Balance School and Sport."

15. Quoted in Kelly Wallace, "SOS for Stressed Out Teens," CNN, December 5, 2013. www.cnn.com.

16. Wallace, "SOS for Stressed Out Teens."

17. Smith, "6 Common Triggers of Teen Stress."

18. Brown, "Life Balance."

19. Toni Bernhard, "4 Tips for Slowing Down to Reduce Stress," *Turning Straw into Gold* (blog), *Psychology Today*, September 13, 2011. www.psychologytoday.com.

Chapter Two: Friendship and Dating

20. Young Men's Health, "Friendship Issues," December 4, 2018. https://youngmenshealthsite.org.

21. American Academy of Pediatrics, "When to Let Your Teenager Start Dating," November 2, 2009. www.healthychildren.org.

22. Newport Academy, "The Importance of Teen Friendship," July 2, 2018. www.newportacademy.com.

23. Quoted in Newport Academy, "The Importance of Teen Friendship."

24. Quoted in American Academy of Pediatrics, "When to Let Your Teenager Start Dating."

25. Quoted in Suzanne M. Wood, "The New Rules for Teen Dating," *Carolina Parent*, April 26, 2018. www.carolinaparent.com.

26. Quoted in American Academy of Pediatrics, "When to Let Your Teenager Start Dating."

27. Wood, "The New Rules for Teen Dating."

28. Quoted in Thurmond, "Under Pressure."

29. Tony Bravo, "What Every LGBT Teen Needs to Know About Dating," *Love & Sex in SF* (blog), SFGate, May 22, 2014. https://blog.sfgate.com.

30. Sheri Madigan et al., "Prevalence of Multiple Forms of Sexting Behavior Among Youth," *JAMA Pediatrics*, April 2018. https://jamanetwork.com.

Chapter Three: Healthy and Unhealthy Body Image

31. Amy Morin, "How to Prevent the Media from Damaging Your Teen's Body Image," *Verywell Family*, January 18, 2019. www.verywellfamily.com.

32. Samantha Phan, "A Story of Body Image," Palo Alto Medical Foundation, 2013. www.pamf.org.

33. Palo Alto Medical Foundation, "Self-Injury and Self-Mutilation," 2013. www.pamf.org.

34. National Eating Disorders Association, "What Are Eating Disorders?," 2018. www.nationaleatingdisorders.org.

35. Quoted in Jen Babakhan, "This Is What It's Really Like to Have Binge Eating Disorder," *Reader's Digest*, 2019. www.rd.com.

36. Quoted in *Office on Women's Health Blog*, "Spotlight on Women's Health," April 29, 2012. www.womenshealth.gov.

37. National Association of Anorexia Nervosa and Associated Disorders, "Eating Disorder Types and Symptoms," 2019. https://anad.org.

38. Julie Saunders, "Stories of Hope: Road to Recovery," National Eating Disorders Association, 2018. www.nationaleatingdisorders.org.

39. National Eating Disorders Association, "Busting the Myths About Eating Disorders," 2018. www.nationaleatingdisorders.org.

40. Costina Papatheodorou, "Tips for Maintaining a Healthy Body Image," Palo Alto Medical Foundation, 2013. www.pamf.org.

Chapter Four: Major Life Transitions

41. Cody Burger, "A Teenager's Story: My Dad Died of Cancer," *Your Teen*, 2019. https://yourteenmag.com.

42. Smith, "6 Common Triggers of Teen Stress."

43. Priya Kshirsagar, "A Story of Transition," Palo Alto Medical Foundation, 2013. www.pamf.org.

44. Drew Adelman, "Life Transitions," Drew Adelman, PhD. http://drewadelman.com.

45. Quoted in Krissy Brady, "If Change Completely Stresses You Out, You Could Have This Disorder," *Self*, July 21, 2016. www.self.com.

46. Quoted in Brady, "If Change Completely Stresses You Out, You Could Have This Disorder."

47. Carl E. Pickhardt, "How Parental Divorce Can Impact Adolescence Now and Later," *Surviving (Your Child's) Adolescence* (blog), *Psychology Today*, November 2, 2015. www.psychologytoday.com.

48. Pickhardt, "How Parental Divorce Can Impact Adolescence Now and Later."

49. Creigh, "My Divorce Story," Divorce and Teens, April 5, 2010. http://divorceandteens.weebly.com.

50. Creigh, "My Divorce Story."

51. Burger, "A Teenager's Story."

52. Alan D. Wolfelt, "Helping Teenagers Cope with Grief," Mercadante Funeral Home & Chapel. www.mercadantefuneral.com.

53. Burger, "A Teenager's Story."

54. Quoted in *Your Teen*, "Coming Out as Gay: A Mother and Son Share Their Story," 2019. https://yourteenmag.com.

55. Quoted in *Your Teen*, "The Coming Out Process: Coming Out Stories from Gay Teens," 2019. https://yourteenmag.com.

56. Quoted in *Your Teen*, "Coming Out as Gay."

57. Quoted in Anna Silman, "10 Teenagers on *Love, Simon* and What It's Actually Like to Come Out in 2018," *The Cut* (blog), *New York*, March 22, 2018. www.thecut.com.

58. Teens Participating in the Summer Wellness Programs, "Emotions and Life," Palo Alto Medical Foundation, 2014. www.pamf.org.

Chapter Five: Signs of Trouble

59. Quoted in Pierre-André Michaud and Eric Fombonne, "Common Mental Health Problems," *BMJ*, April 9, 2005. www.ncbi.nlm.nih.gov.

60. Michaud and Fombonne, "Common Mental Health Problems."
61. Todd Callahan, "Anxiety," Young Men's Health, May 11, 2017. https://youngmenshealthsite.org.
62. Alicia Tatar, "What Anxiety in Teens Looks and Feels Like: Alicia's Story," *Your Teen*, 2019. https://yourteenmag.com.
63. Mental Health America, "Depression in Teens," 2019. www.mentalhealthamerica.net.
64. Topanga Brown, "Sink the Stigma," Anxiety and Depression Association of America. https://adaa.org.
65. Quoted in Young Men's Health, "I've Been Having Depression and Anxiety Problems for 3 Years," September 29, 2016. https://youngmenshealthsite.org.
66. Todd Callahan, "ADHD," Young Men's Health, May 4, 2018. https://youngmenshealthsite.org.
67. Quoted in Leslie Alderman, "Living with ADHD: Max's Story," Everyday Health, August 31, 2010. www.everydayhealth.com.
68. Savannah, "True Story: Savannah," Phoenix House, October 2, 2012. www.phoenixhouse.org.
69. Brown, "Sink the Stigma."

FOR FURTHER RESEARCH

Books

Gina Biegel and Breanna Chambers, *Take in the Good: Skills for Staying Positive and Living Your Best Life*. Boulder, CO: Shambhala, 2019.

Jeffrey Cheng, *Sam's Journal: A Powerful Journey Towards Mental Health Through Prose, Poetry, and Pictures*. Charleston, SC: Amazon Digital Services, 2018.

Carmen Cusido, *Coping with Eating Disorders*. New York: Rosen, 2019.

Grace Griffin, *Creating Happy: How I Survived High School with Social Anxiety Disorder*. Charleston, SC: Amazon Digital Services, 2018.

Paul L. Hemphill, *Inspiration for Teens: 88 True Stories with Life Lessons*. Charleston, SC: Amazon Digital Services, 2018.

Amy Newmark, *Think Positive for Teens*. Cos Cob, CT: Chicken Soup for the Soul, 2019.

Brook Waters, *Be You: A Teenage Depression Workbook*. Scotts Valley, CA: CreateSpace, 2018.

Sara Woods, *Identifying as Transgender*. New York: Rosen, 2017.

Internet Sources

Anna Brown, "5 Key Findings About LGBT Americans," Pew Research Center, June 13, 2017. www.pewresearch.org.

Sherri Gordon, "5 Ways to Help Your Teen Navigate Social Media During a Breakup," Verywell Family, March 12, 2018. www.very wellfamily.com.

Rachel Hills, "4 People Explain What It's Like Being Genderqueer," *Cosmopolitan*, April 28, 2017. www.cosmopolitan.com.

Crystal Karges, "How Eating Disorders Can Affect Relationships," Eating Disorder Hope, February 25, 2017. www.eatingdisorder hope.com.

Amy Morin, "How to Prevent the Media from Damaging Your Teen's Body Image," Verywell Family, January 18, 2019. www.verywellfamily.com.

National Institute of Mental Health, "Eating Disorders Among Children," 2018. www.nimh.nih.gov.

Barbara Poncelet, "Male Body Issues in Teens That All Parents Should Know," Verywell Family, March 13, 2019. www.verywell family.com.

Teens Against Bullying, "Real Teens Speak Out," 2019. https://pacerteensagainstbullying.org.

TeensHealth, "Depression," 2016. https://kidshealth.org.

Websites

Teen Mental Health, Medline Plus (https://medlineplus.gov/teenmentalhealth.html). This extremely useful website contains dozens of links to articles of varied lengths about related topics, such as the latest statistics on teens' mental health, diagnosis of various common mental issues teens face, danger signs of illness, how to find professional help, and much more.

Tips for Maintaining a Healthy Body Image, Palo Alto Medical Foundation (www.pamf.org/teen/life/bodyimage/healthy image.html). This comprehensive site presents wide-ranging information on how teens can maintain a healthy body image, from proper diet to exercise to avoiding illegal drugs, and more. Links lead to fuller discussions of several of the issues involved.

Transgender FAQ, GLAAD (www.glaad.org/transgender/trans faq). The noted human rights organization GLAAD presents this well-written, informative overview of transgenderism, explaining to teens and others the basic concepts, along with links to articles about related issues.

American Academy of Child & Adolescent Psychiatry (AACAP)
3615 Wisconsin Ave. NW
Washington, DC 20016-3007
website: www.aacap.org

AACAP's mission is to promote the health of children, adolescents, and families. On the group's website, teens can find lists of doctors and other health care professionals in their areas, as well as a section—illustrated by cartoons—telling what it is like to visit such doctors.

National Alliance on Mental Illness (NAMI)
3803 N. Fairfax Dr., Suite 100
Arlington, VA 22203
website: www.nami.org

NAMI is a foundation linking hundreds of organizations that help people suffering from various forms of mental illness. The website has a 24/7 hotline, along with links to articles that provide teens with advice about what to do if they or members of their family need help.

National Center for Transgender Equality (NCTE)
1133 Nineteenth St. NW, Suite 302
Washington, DC 20036
website: http://transequality.org

The NCTE's mission is to help trans teens and other trans people enjoy equality and social justice. The group's website features sections that explain to young people the complexities of what transgenderism actually is, along with updates on changing laws that affect trans teens.

National Eating Disorders Association (NEDA)

165 W. Forty-Sixth St., Suite 402

New York, NY 10036

website: www.nationaleatingdisorders.org

NEDA supports teens and their family members, as well as others affected by eating disorders, and promotes prevention of those disorders. The NEDA website provides a national help line, along with articles and blogs written by teens who describe their struggles with eating disorders.

National Institute of Mental Health (NIMH)

6001 Executive Blvd., Room 6200, MSC 9663

Bethesda, MD 20892-9663

website: www.nimh.nih.gov

NIMH is the leading federal agency for research on mental disorders. For teenagers seeking help, the NIMH website contains information about depression, anxiety disorders, eating disorders, suicide prevention, and other similar issues and suggests ways to find help.

PFLAG

1828 L St., Suite 660

Washington, DC 20036

website: www.pflag.org

PFLAG works on behalf of the interests of LBGT people everywhere. The PFLAG website features a locator that teens can use to find the closest of the group's more than four hundred chapters nationwide. The site also tells LGBT teens how they can better their lives in a section titled "Make My Voice Heard."

Power to Decide

1776 Massachusetts Ave. NW, Suite 200

Washington, DC 20036

website: www.thenationalcampaign.org

Power to Decide (formerly the National Campaign to Prevent Teen and Unplanned Pregnancy) promotes responsible behavior by teens in sexual matters in order to reduce the occurrence of unplanned pregnancies. The group's website contains sections with advice on healthy relationships, abstinence, contraception, and how teens can talk to their doctors.

Substance Abuse and Mental Health Services Administration (SAMHSA)

5600 Fishers Ln.
Rockville, MD 20852
website: www.samhsa.gov

SAMHSA's mission is to reduce the impact of substance abuse and mental illness in American schools and communities. Its website provides a national help line that teens can call if they seek aid, plus a "services locator" that directs them to clinics in their areas.

INDEX

PICTURE CREDITS

ABOUT THE AUTHOR

In addition to his numerous acclaimed volumes on ancient civilizations, historian Don Nardo has published several studies of medical and scientific discoveries and phenomena, including *Vaccines*, *Biomedical Ethics*, *Nanotechnology and Medicine*, *The Scientific Revolution*, *Science and Sustainable Energy*, and award-winning books on astronomy and space exploration. Nardo also composes and arranges orchestral music. He lives with his wife, Christine, in Massachusetts.